One day, Worm went to the woods
to gather walnuts.
He brought his wagon with him.

On his way home, Worm saw Woodpecker
whistling in a weeping willow.
Woodpecker asked Worm for a ride.

Worm wiggled along, pulling Woodpecker
in his wagon. Soon they came upon Weasel
eating watermelon.
Weasel asked Worm for a ride.

Worm wiggled along, pulling Woodpecker and Weasel in his wagon. Before long, they bumped into Wombat wearing her new wig. Wombat asked Worm for a ride.

Worm wiggled along, pulling Woodpecker,
Weasel, and Wombat in his wagon.
Next, they met Wolf on his way to work.
Wolf asked Worm for a ride.

Worm wiggled along, pulling Woodpecker,
Weasel, Wombat, and Wolf in his wagon.
Soon they saw Walrus winking and waving.
Walrus asked Worm for a ride.

Worm wiggled along, pulling Woodpecker, Weasel, Wombat, Wolf, and Walrus in his wagon. Up ahead, they saw Whale playing in the water. Whale asked Worm for a ride.

Worm wiggled with all his might trying to pull
Woodpecker, Weasel, Wombat, Wolf, Walrus,
and Whale in the wagon. But the wagon
would not move. The wheels started to wobble.

8

WHAM!
The weight was too much for the wagon.
It crashed to the ground.
"Oh, no! My wagon!" Worm wailed.

"Don't worry, Worm," the animals said.

Worm's friends worked on the wagon all afternoon.

When the wagon was fixed,
Worm wiggled into it.

Then Wombat, Weasel, Wolf, Woodpecker,
Walrus, and Whale pulled Worm all the way home.
And weary Worm had a wonderful ride.

See inside back cover for answers.

Ww Cheer

W is for worm and a wagon to pull

W is for wig, whale, wave, and wool

W is for watermelon, juicy and sweet

W is for walnuts, waffles, and wheat

Hooray for **W**, big and small—

the wildest, wackiest letter of all!